# FROM DEBT TO WEALTH

## MANAGING PERSONAL FINANCE

**MARY AYISI BOADU**

authorHOUSE®

*AuthorHouse™ UK*
*1663 Liberty Drive*
*Bloomington, IN 47403 USA*
*www.authorhouse.co.uk*
*Phone: 0800.197.4150*

*© 2019 Mary Ayisi Boadu. All rights reserved.*

*No part of this book may be reproduced, stored in a retrieval system, or transmitted by any means without the written permission of the author.*

*Scripture quotations marked NASB are taken from the New American Standard Bible®, Copyright © 1960, 1962, 1963, 1968, 1971, 1972, 1973, 1975, 1977, 1995 by HYPERLINK "http://www.lockman.org/" The Lockman Foundation. Used by HYPERLINK "http://www.lockman.org/tlf/copyright.php"permission.*

*Scripture quotations marked KJV are from the Holy Bible, King James Version (Authorized Version). First published in 1611. Quoted from the KJV Classic Reference Bible, Copyright © 1983 by The HYPERLINK "http://www.zondervan.com/" Zondervan Corporation.*

*Scripture quotations marked NIV are taken from the Holy Bible, New International Version®. NIV®. Copyright © 1973, 1978, 1984 by International Bible Society. Used by permission of HYPERLINK "http://www.zondervan.com/" Zondervan. All rights reserved. [ HYPERLINK "http://www.biblica.com/niv/" Biblica]*

*Published by AuthorHouse 04/08/2019*

*ISBN: 978-1-7283-8688-1 (sc)*
*ISBN: 978-1-7283-8689-8 (e)*

*Print information available on the last page.*

*Any people depicted in stock imagery provided by Getty Images are models, and such images are being used for illustrative purposes only. Certain stock imagery © Getty Images.*

*This book is printed on acid-free paper.*

*Because of the dynamic nature of the Internet, any web addresses or links contained in this book may have changed since publication and may no longer be valid. The views expressed in this work are solely those of the author and do not necessarily reflect the views of the publisher, and the publisher hereby disclaims any responsibility for them.*

I dedicate this book to my late mother, Mrs Augustina Ayisi. Your hard work has paid off. I wish you were here to enjoy the fruit of your labour. Love you always.

I also dedicate the book to my husband, Nick, and my three beautiful daughters, Nicole, Kelly-Louise, and Mikayla. Thank you all for your patience in letting me be when I was busily working on this book and you kind of felt ignored. I appreciate you all, and I pray that the subject of debt stops here and will not overflow to the next generations.

# PREFACE

I have always had the desire to write a book on finance, but that I couldn't do it before because I was heavily indebted to my bank. One day I was having a discussion with my ex-manager, and the topic of debt and wealth came up. I had guilt written all over my face, and so he asked if my finances were in order. At that point there was no denying it, and I said I had a credit card with a balance on it which I was trying to pay off. He asked me the balance on the credit card, and I said it was ten thousand pounds. I was thinking of the credit limit, but he'd asked about the balance on the card. Even though I had not fully used up all the funds to the limit, I had a sizeable balance on the card and could not account for the usage.

I later reflected on our conversation and realised I had mismanaged my credit, which had to be put right.

# CONTENTS

Introduction ................................................................ xi
Taking Control of Your Finances ..................................... 1
Why Are People Always Broke? ........................................ 3
Differences between Average and Wealthy People ........... 7
Needs versus wants .......................................................... 8
So What Is Debt? ............................................................. 9
Five Principles of Money Solution ..................................10
    Principles Of Giving ..................................................14
Pay off Debt ...................................................................16
    How to Pay off Debt and Build Wealth ....................17
    Are You Ready to Pay off Your Debts and Invest? ....19
Credit Score and Credit Report—How Do They Work?... 27
    What Is a Credit Score? ............................................ 27
    How Does a Credit Score Work? .............................. 28
    What Does Your Experian Credit Score Mean
    for You? ................................................................... 28
    What Is a Credit Report? ......................................... 29
    Where Does the Information in Your Credit
    Report Come From? .................................................31
    When Should You Check Your Credit Report? ........31
    How To Improve Your Credit Score ........................ 32

- What the Rich Do with Their Money............................ 36
- What Is Investment? ....................................................... 39
  - Risk and Return ...................................................... 40
  - Investing and Saving................................................ 40
  - Types of Investments............................................... 41
  - Bonds....................................................................... 42
  - Alternative Investments........................................... 42
  - Investing for Income and Growth: Predictable Returns versus Growing in Value ............................ 43
  - Risk Appetite: How Much Uncertainty Would You Comfortably Accept?............................ 43
  - Life Stages: Time, the Young Investor's Friend ........ 44
  - Life Stages: Midlife ..................................................45
  - Life Stages: Preretirement Income ...........................45
  - Life Stages: Postretirement Income ......................... 46
- A Sturdy Flow of Income? .............................................. 47
- What Are Mutual Funds?................................................ 49
  - Types of Mutual Funds............................................ 50
  - Advantages and Disadvantages of Mutual Funds .....51
  - Mutual Funds Fees .................................................. 52
  - Buying and Selling of Mutual Funds ....................... 53
- Investing in Properties......................................................61
  - Why Invest in Properties? ........................................ 62
  - Types of Property Investments ................................ 63
- Investments..................................................................... 66
- How to Save Money the Unconventional Way .............. 67
- Smart Money, Wise Kids—Let's Not Forget Our Children........................................................................... 69
- The Power of Compound Interest .................................. 71

- Glossary of information ................................................. 89
- Endnotes ..........................................................................91

# INTRODUCTION

Financial education was never taught in schools no matter which country you lived in or which school you attended. Most of us grew up not knowing how to manage our own finances. Some people earn a lot of money but end up wasting a lot of it, having nothing left at the end of the month. We save less or have nothing left at all, and even if we save money, we end up withdrawing money from our savings accounts and spend it unnecessarily. We buy things we do not need, borrow money from banks, and mismanage our funds. We have no vision of having a passive income or managing the resources we already have, so how on earth do we expect to be wealthy?

The first key to becoming wealthy is to understand and hold a belief that you already are wealthy. Re-evaluate your financial situation and find strategies to manage your finances.

As soon as you begin planning for your family, you should take your financial planning seriously because having children comes with extra expenditure. When your children start nursery, primary school, or university, you will need money to support them. When your children want to get married, it would be nice to support them financially too. When your children are buying a house but do not have enough money, it would be great to help them with their deposit money.

When you or your children are sick and you need medical care, how do you pay for the doctor? If your family is hungry and you need to give them food, what does it take to feed them? In retirement, who will look after you?

When you have to dress your children and send them to school to educate them, what does it take? Is it not the same money that will look after you? Money will not make you happy, but lack of money will certainly make you miserable, so it is about time we find out how to manage and save money for our future.

This book will help you pause and think whether what you are about to spend your money on is worth it. You can make a wise and conscious decision to invest money, which will compound and accumulate over years. We should educate our children so their finances will also be healthy in the long term.

# TAKING CONTROL OF YOUR FINANCES

If you want to take control of your finances, you have to be realistic about your income and expenditures, purely looking at them in black and white. The first step to taking total control of your finances is to assess your current financial situation. To start this, you need to jot down all your monthly income and expenditures. This gives you a clear picture of how much inflow you receive and your spending situation. Make sure you include all the purchases you make on debit and credit cards, even small amounts like twenty pence, because smaller amounts have a way of mounting up quickly. Also include the bills you pay by cheque or direct debit. You need to update this record every day and total the amounts at the end of the month.

You must check whether you have bad patterns in your spending habits. For example, do you withdraw a huge amount of money from your account on payday and spend it unnecessarily? Is your spending worse on weekdays or weekends? Do you spend a lot on Friday night out with friends and colleagues, or does this all happen during your lunch hour, when you visit the shops and end up with bags of shopping? Nobody wants to waste money, but we do it unknowingly or without proper planning. Keeping a spending diary will help you identify your spending weaknesses and measure what they really cost.

By building on your spending diary, you are ready to take a broader look at your personal money flow. You will need all your bank statements and credit card bills for the last year. Get a calculator. Gather any unpaid bills and your latest statements from your savings, mortgage, and pension providers. Fill in the income and expenditure statement on the last pages of this book. If your income varies from month to month, add up last year's total and divide by twelve months.

Do not forget to include anyone you share finances with—for example, your wife, husband, or significant other.

# WHY ARE PEOPLE ALWAYS BROKE?

Everybody is born talented, but not all people use their talents to their benefit. Many people cannot identify their talents, and so they go on in life doing menial jobs with incomes that barely get them through the month.

Even when they can't afford it, people buy brand-new cars on credit that lose value as soon as they leave the dealership. Some of you buy a Louis Vuitton bag at £1,000–5,000 when your rent is due and you have no house of your own. Too many people carry too much debt and don't live within their means. Instead, they try to impress people who don't even like them or care what they do. Pampering yourself is good, but do not indulge too much in it. Don't worry about getting your hair and nails done at the expense of your kids' educations or your investments for old age. Building funds for your pension is key.

People do not budget. They simply spend, living from pay cheque to pay cheque. When you do a written budget, it makes you live within your means. A written budget, when properly laid out, will make you think that you've got a pay increase or have been promoted with a better income.

When you are faithful with the little, you will be given more to manage, so write out your budget and stick to it. You will make progress with your finances when you start budgeting. When you have a written budget and stick to it in a disciplined way, you will have excess funds to clear your debt if you have any.

People don't pay their bills on time simply because of poor organisation or not developing a simple strategy to cater to those bills. The best advice is to not make it complicated. Simply write it down in a notebook and pay it immediately. Or you can put it on direct debit for funds to go out when your account is in credit. Prioritise your bills and communicate with creditors you're not able to pay so that they are aware of your situation. Some companies send monthly reports to credit reference bureaus, and these are the ones you want to quickly honour. The consequences of not paying can damage your credit score and credibility.

A lot of things are purchased with the hope of getting money in the future to settle the bills. No one can predict the future, so never buy things you cannot afford now. Don't buy things on credit cards either. Failure to honour your payment will destroy your credit ratings with the credit reference agencies. Bad credit will make potential mortgage lenders deny you good home or car loans. Even if they are willing to help, they will offer this assistance with high interest rates. Don't stay broke by overspending and not saving for future life events because this could depress you.

When you are responsible with your credit, your children will copy your lifestyle. This will help them in their adult lives to avoid debt and be disciplined.

Too many credit cards will lead to bad credit because the availability of funds will overwhelm you. You'll be more likely to misuse the cards, negatively affecting your credit score. A bad credit score can wreak havoc in many areas of your life. With bad credit, you will not qualify for new credit such as loans and mortgages. It can prevent you from getting a job or even make you lose your job because some employers, especially in the financial industries, do annual credit checks on their employees. The status of your credit report gives the lender a view of how dependable you could be in the future. With a bad credit score, you may not be able to rent a home. It can also prevent you from getting homeowners' insurance.

Most people do not have an emergency fund and resort to borrowing when the inevitable happens. Life is full of surprises, and that is why you need an emergency fund. You need to save between six to eight months of your monthly expenses. Start today with what you can afford and build it up to 15 per cent of your monthly income. A helpful tip is to take advantage of automatic deposit.

Use emergency funds only for true emergencies, like health, essential expenses, and home and car loans. When used, replenish the account so it will be available for your next emergency.

*Things to Remember*

Broke people are not givers because they are highly in debt and cannot afford to give.

People do not have written goals. Work with and constantly refer to your goals. Make sure you are on track.

Many people do not educate and upgrade themselves. In this case, I'm talking about self-education, not formal education. You tend to learn and absorb more information when you research and learn it yourself.

Don't spend your whole life chasing money and ignoring yourself, family, and social life. But don't stay broke by overspending and not saving for future life events because this could depress you.

# DIFFERENCES BETWEEN AVERAGE AND WEALTHY PEOPLE

Average people work for money month in and month out. They spend the money and look forward to the next payday. They have a scarcity mentality: everything is so difficult to get and so scarce that they have to work harder to get anything. Average people talk themselves out of prosperity, leading to the disempowerment of their mentality. Average people learn financial behaviours from their parents, disregarding self-education. Average people exhibit so much fear that it prevents them from taking key actions.

On the other hand, wealthy people have an abundance mentality. They don't work for money; they invest in assets which will generate income for them for their lifetimes so that money ends up working for them. Wealthy people ask the right questions and learn their financial behaviours from experts. Wealthy people have the same fears as average people, but they do things anyway. They do not allow fear to hold them back.

# **NEEDS VERSUS WANTS**

Do you have an eight-month emergency fund? Are you funding your retirement account? Do you have credit card debt and are paying interest on it? Are you behind on payments? Do you have a student loan in deferment or default? You'd better get serious with your life because you know what a want and a need are. Most student loans are not dischargeable in court, and so you can never run away from repayments; they will hang around your neck until repaid. Remember that you need money to go to the grocery store and buy food, not money to dine at a restaurant. You need petrol in your car to get to work, not petrol for clubbing and parties. You can fool around with money all you want, but at the end of the day, the only person you are hurting is yourself. If you don't have money, you should only buy something you need, not because you want it. Do not go broke trying to look rich.

# SO WHAT IS DEBT?

Debt is surely not a sin, but it is dangerous. Debt is like a prison because it puts people into emotional prison. Debt creates fear of the future, tension, apprehension, and an environment of stress. Debt can be likened to a cancer that destroys marriages and homes. Debt leads parents into drinking and alcoholism, and hence child abuse. Debt can even separate you from your family.

Debt is not a good thing to have and should not be entertained in our lives. If you have an attitude of compulsive spending, you need deliverance.

# FIVE PRINCIPLES OF MONEY SOLUTION

Get out of debt.

The Bible says that the rich rules over the poor, and the borrower is slave to the lender (Proverbs 22:7).

Rip up your credit cards, and never get them again.

Don't buy stuff you don't have money for.

Don't buy things you don't need.

Imagine how much you can save or invest if you don't have any card payments.

2. Act your wage.

Only live on the money you make. Don't spend all you make. The Bible says Godliness with contentment is great gain (1 Timothy 6:6–11).

3. Get on a budget.

Control yourself. Luke 14:28 HYPERLINK "https://biblehub.com/nasb/luke/14.htm" New American Standard Bible states, "For which one of you, when he wants to build a tower, does not first sit down and calculate the cost to see if he has enough to complete it?"

4. Learn to save money.

Save for an emergency fund. So long as we live, things will happen. You need at least six months' emergency money in your savings.

Proverbs 21:20 HYPERLINK "https://biblehub.com/kjv/proverbs/21.htm" King James Bible says, "There is treasure to be desired and oil in the dwelling of the wise; but a foolish man spendeth it up."

Save to pay cash because it will make you spend less. You spend more with debit or credit cards than you will do with cash.

Debt is not a sin but is biblically stupid.

When you save money, you invest money. Invest for your future. Invest for your kids' college.

*From Debt to Wealth*

5. Give. With debt, you don't have enough to be a giver.

## PRINCIPLES OF GIVING

In everything I did, I showed you that by this kind of hard work we must help the weak, remembering the words the Lord Jesus himself said: "It is more blessed to give than to receive." (Acts 20:35) HYPERLINK "https://biblehub.com/kjv/proverbs/21.htm" King James Bible

If a brother or sister is without clothing and in need of daily food, and one of you says to them, "Go in peace, be warmed and be filled," and yet you do not give them what is necessary for their body, what use is that? James 2:15–16 HYPERLINK "https://biblehub.com/nasb/luke/14.htm" New American Standard Bible

"Bring the whole tithe into the storehouse, that there may be food in my house. Test me in this," says the LORD Almighty, "and see if I will not throw open the floodgates of heaven and pour out so much blessing that you will not have room enough for it." (Malachi 3:10) HYPERLINK "https://biblehub.com/niv/malachi/3.htm" New International Version

Now concerning the collection for the saints, as I directed the churches of Galatia, so do you also. On the first day of every week each one of you is to put aside and save, as he may prosper, so that no collections be made when I come. (1 Corinthians 16:1–2)

But when you do a charitable deed, do not let your left hand know what your right hand is doing, that your charitable deed may be in secret; and your Father who sees in secret will Himself reward you openly. (Matthew 6:3–4)

And he would answer and say to them, "The man who has two tunics is to share with him who has none; and he who has food is to do likewise." (Luke 3:11) HYPERLINK "https://biblehub.com/nasb/luke/3.htm" New American Standard Bible

Now He who supplies seed to the sower and bread for food will supply and multiply your seed for sowing and increase the harvest of your righteousness. (2 Corinthians 9:10) HYPERLINK "https://biblehub.com/nasb/luke/3.htm" New American Standard Bible

Give, and it will be given to you. They will pour into your lap a good measure, pressed down, shaken together, and running over. For by your standard of measure it will be measured to you in return. (Luke 6:38) HYPERLINK "https://biblehub.com/nasb/luke/3.htm" New American Standard Bible

# PAY OFF DEBT

Sadly, many people have more debt than savings—if they have any savings at all. They pay so much in interest, which is barely clearing their loan. Imagine if you did not have any debt payment in this world, and all the money you earned was yours. For some, it will free up anywhere between one hundred and one thousand pounds, if not more. Most people manage to pay enough to meet the minimum payment requirement each month leaving the balance of the debt as it is.

In order to start saving money, paying off your debt is key. In order to do this, you need to have a plan and a budget in place. To clear off debt, write them down, listing the ones with the highest interest rate first. However, to start repaying your debt, pay off the smallest debt high interest first to give you motivation in your debt repayments. It is very important to have a strategy of debt repayment that gives you the motivation to complete what you have planned and started to do. This always happens when you pay off the smallest debt with higher interest. Strike-through the amount to confirm that it is repaid.

You could make minimum repayments on all of your debt except the smallest with higher interest, which you have to throw more money at to reduce it. Once this smallest with higher interest is paid off, apply funds to the next debt whilst you continue to make minimum payments for the rest. The more you pay off your debt, the more your freed-up money grows, giving you enough for your repayments. Repeat this payment strategy until all your debt is paid off.

When you're debt free, you are able to live and give.

## HOW TO PAY OFF DEBT AND BUILD WEALTH

Paying off your debt can sometimes be stressful if you don't know how to do it properly. Some people will consider all kinds of options like bankruptcy or IVA if you live in the United Kingdom. Some will even consider debt consolidation but will accept offers even if it's at a higher interest rate.

To pay off your debt, you need to be strategic and tactical. Have a radical solution approach to trade off a short-term pain and discomfort for your long-term comfort. Short-term pain will give you your long-term peace of mind.

You need a written budget every month before the month begins. Write down your income and expenditure and look to your reallocation of funds. Budgeting will give you an idea of what your expected income for the month is and your expenditure. Reconsider the bills that you can eliminate temporarily or permanently—for example, gym membership or a very expensive vehicle.

Cancel subscriptions such as magazines, Sky TV, or cable if you can.

Most people are light users on mobile phone units. Reconsider your mobile phone contract.

If you have things you don't often use, do a garage sale to release money and reduce your debt.

Reduce the number of times you eat out. Eat at home, take packed lunches to work, and be strict with yourself. Remember that you are trading off short-term pain for a long-term gain. Quit buying expensive beverages and lattes every single day because it adds up to your expenditure. You could make this at home and take to work, or have it in powdered form and make it at work. Stop going to the movies and find another way of entertaining yourself for the short time you are paying off your debt.

Reduce utilities wherever possible. It's better to keep your money than to give it to some company. Consciously turn off lights when you leave a room. Take a shower instead of a bath.

Stick to a strict weekly food budget. Drink plenty of water instead of other beverages. Most beverages are too expensive and might not even be good for your health because they are loaded with sugar and preservatives.

If you don't have pets, please wait because pet ownership can be very expensive. Their food, grooming, and insurances are so expensive.

If visiting shops makes you overspend, shop online and only buy what you need.

Paying off debt means you control your spending. You stick to it and do not waver.

## ARE YOU READY TO PAY OFF YOUR DEBTS AND INVEST?

For those who want to be guided in wealth building, you can follow the below steps to pay off your debts and gradually climb up in wealth creation.

Step 1 is to create your first thousand pounds of emergency fund as a buffer that will support you in case you meet a bump in the road. This is like a starter fund but will give you the peace of mind that you have something small tucked away in the bank untouched. If you have this emergency fund in place, you will not run to your credit card when in need.

Step 2 is to get out of debt and stay out of it. Remember that debt comes with stress, regret, and shame and will destroy your retirement dream. Be prepared to settle all your debt in the order described above, from smallest to largest. Use all the income you have and get out of it as quickly as possible. Make paying off your debt your priority. Remember that when you pay off your debt and stay out of debt, it frees up your largest wealth-building tool, which is your income. Once your debts are paid off, you won't be scared of your creditors, and you are able to throw more money into your investments.

Step 3 is to build a full three- to six-month emergency fund. Once you're able to pay off all your debt with the exception of your mortgage, you can follow on from step one and build a full emergency fund to cover expenses. Imagine the feeling when you have no debt but a savings of twenty thousand pounds sitting in the bank

Step 4 is to save 10–20 per cent in your retirement account. Attack your retirement dream with a passion by finding all the tax-favoured retirement plans. Make good use of corporate-matching retirement savings schemes because you end up getting free money when companies match your contributions.

Step 5 is to save for your children's colleges and universities. However, your retirement contributions take priority because retirement is sure to happen, whereas a child continuing education to the university level is not guaranteed, and children will be able to work and pay for at least part of it themselves.

Step 6 is where you pay off the house you live in. Remember that steps 4, 5, and 6 will all happen at the same time. Say that extra funds will go towards reducing your mortgage. Your home mortgage is the biggest debt, but it's the last in your journey of debt payment. Once the house is fully paid off, then you will be 100 per cent debt free. Can you picture this happening in the near future? Can you picture how liberating that will feel? I can see the smiles on your face already.

At this point, step 7, you are debt free. You do not run away from your creditors, and you have a big emergency fund sitting in your bank account for just in case you need them. You are on track towards contributing to your retirement account, and your children's college or university savings are all in order. Then you can focus more on building your retirement wealth dream. This is the time that you build wealth to change your family, your community, and your legacy for your generations. Now is the best time to practice extreme generosity and advise others on wealth building through the avoidance of debt. For example, if you are aged twenty-five years and are able to save one thousand pounds monthly at an investment rate of 10 per cent (over time) for a period of forty years, with the help of compound interest (which adds interest on principal), it will roll and add on and keep rolling, and you will have over six million pounds in your investment account at the end of that period. This illustration is only assuming you earn a lot or your expenditure is low and can save more.

| Year | Beginning Balance | Interest (10%) | Total Interest | Additions (£1,000 Monthly) | Total Additions | Ending Balance |
|---|---|---|---|---|---|---|
| 1 | £1,000.00 | £104.71 | £670.28 | £12,000.00 | £12,000.00 | £13,670.28 |
| 2 | £13,670.28 | £220.39 | £2,667.31 | £12,000.00 | £24,000.00 | £27,667.31 |
| 3 | £27,667.31 | £348.18 | £6,130.00 | £12,000.00 | £36,000.00 | £43,130.00 |
| 4 | £43,130.00 | £489.35 | £11,211.85 | £12,000.00 | £48,000.00 | £60,211.85 |
| 5 | £60,211.85 | £645.31 | £18,082.38 | £12,000.00 | £60,000.00 | £79,082.38 |
| 6 | £79,082.38 | £817.59 | £26,928.91 | £12,000.00 | £72,000.00 | £99,928.91 |
| 7 | £99,928.91 | £1,007.92 | £37,958.34 | £12,000.00 | £84,000.00 | £122,958.34 |
| 8 | £122,958.34 | £1,218.18 | £51,399.25 | £12,000.00 | £96,000.00 | £148,399.25 |
| 9 | £148,399.25 | £1,450.45 | £67,504.16 | £12,000.00 | £108,000.00 | £176,504.16 |
| 10 | £176,504.16 | £1,707.04 | £86,552.02 | £12,000.00 | £120,000.00 | £207,552.02 |
| 11 | £207,552.02 | £1,990.50 | £108,851.00 | £12,000.00 | £132,000.00 | £241,851.00 |
| 12 | £241,851.00 | £2,303.65 | £134,741.53 | £12,000.00 | £144,000.00 | £279,741.53 |
| 13 | £279,741.53 | £2,649.58 | £164,599.69 | £12,000.00 | £156,000.00 | £321,599.69 |
| 14 | £321,599.69 | £3,031.74 | £198,840.94 | £12,000.00 | £168,000.00 | £367,840.94 |
| 15 | £367,840.94 | £3,453.92 | £237,924.27 | £12,000.00 | £180,000.00 | £418,924.27 |
| 16 | £418,924.27 | £3,920.30 | £282,356.68 | £12,000.00 | £192,000.00 | £475,356.68 |

| Year | Beginning Balance | Interest (10%) | Total Interest | Additions (£1,000 Monthly) | Total Additions | Ending Balance |
|---|---|---|---|---|---|---|
| 17 | £475,356.68 | £4,435.52 | £332,698.30 | £12,000.00 | £204,000.00 | £537,698.30 |
| 18 | £537,698.30 | £5,004.69 | £389,567.91 | £12,000.00 | £216,000.00 | £606,567.91 |
| 19 | £606,567.91 | £5,633.46 | £453,649.06 | £12,000.00 | £228,000.00 | £682,649.06 |
| 20 | £682,649.06 | £6,328.07 | £525,696.91 | £12,000.00 | £240,000.00 | £766,696.91 |
| 21 | £766,696.91 | £7,095.42 | £606,545.66 | £12,000.00 | £252,000.00 | £859,545.66 |
| 22 | £859,545.66 | £7,943.11 | £697,116.89 | £12,000.00 | £264,000.00 | £962,116.89 |
| 23 | £962,116.89 | £8,879.58 | £798,428.67 | £12,000.00 | £276,000.00 | £1,075,428.67 |
| 24 | £1,075,428.67 | £9,914.10 | £911,605.68 | £12,000.00 | £288,000.00 | £1,200,605.68 |
| 25 | £1,200,605.68 | £11,056.95 | £1,037,890.35 | £12,000.00 | £300,000.00 | £1,338,890.35 |
| 26 | £1,338,890.35 | £12,319.46 | £1,178,655.23 | £12,000.00 | £312,000.00 | £1,491,655.23 |
| 27 | £1,491,655.23 | £13,714.19 | £1,335,416.59 | £12,000.00 | £324,000.00 | £1,660,416.59 |
| 28 | £1,660,416.59 | £15,254.95 | £1,509,849.48 | £12,000.00 | £336,000.00 | £1,846,849.48 |
| 29 | £1,846,849.48 | £16,957.06 | £1,703,804.32 | £12,000.00 | £348,000.00 | £2,052,804.32 |
| 30 | £2,052,804.32 | £18,837.40 | £1,919,325.32 | £12,000.00 | £360,000.00 | £2,280,325.32 |
| 31 | £2,280,325.32 | £20,914.63 | £2,158,670.75 | £12,000.00 | £372,000.00 | £2,531,670.75 |
| 32 | £2,531,670.75 | £23,209.38 | £2,424,335.33 | £12,000.00 | £384,000.00 | £2,809,335.33 |
| 33 | £2,809,335.33 | £25,744.42 | £2,719,075.02 | £12,000.00 | £396,000.00 | £3,116,075.02 |

| Year | Beginning Balance | Interest (10%) | Total Interest | Additions (£1,000 Monthly) | Total Additions | Ending Balance |
|---|---|---|---|---|---|---|
| 34 | £3,116,075.02 | £28,544.91 | £3,045,934.36 | £12,000.00 | £408,000.00 | £3,454,934.36 |
| 35 | £3,454,934.36 | £31,638.65 | £3,408,276.70 | £12,000.00 | £420,000.00 | £3,829,276.70 |
| 36 | £3,829,276.70 | £35,056.34 | £3,809,817.58 | £12,000.00 | £432,000.00 | £4,242,817.58 |
| 37 | £4,242,817.58 | £38,831.91 | £4,254,661.59 | £12,000.00 | £444,000.00 | £4,699,661.59 |
| 38 | £4,699,661.59 | £43,002.84 | £4,747,343.14 | £12,000.00 | £456,000.00 | £5,204,343.14 |
| 39 | £5,204,343.14 | £47,610.51 | £5,292,871.44 | £12,000.00 | £468,000.00 | £5,761,871.44 |
| 40 | £6,324,079.58 | £52,700.66 | £5,896,780.24 | £12,000.00 | £480,000.00 | £6,377,780.24 |

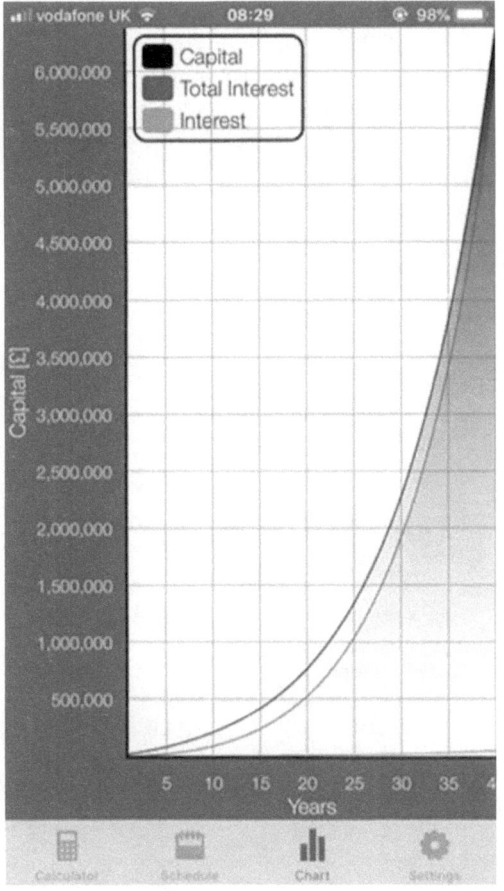

## Calculator

### INPUTS

| | | |
|---|---|---|
| Principal | | £1,000.00 |
| Interest | | 10 % |
| Compound | | Monthly |
| Duration | 40 | Years |
| Additions | ± £1,000.00 | Monthly |
| | | at end of period |

### RESULTS

| | |
|---|---|
| Total Interest | £5,896,780.24 |
| Total Additions | £480,000.00 |
| Ending Balance | £6,377,780.24 |

# CREDIT SCORE AND CREDIT REPORT—HOW DO THEY WORK?

## WHAT IS A CREDIT SCORE?[12]

A credit score is a number that reflects the likelihood of you paying back credit. Lenders like banks and credit card companies will look at your credit history when they calculate your credit score, which will show them the level of risk in lending to you. The higher your credit score, the better chance of being accepted for credit at the best rates.

Your credit score influences your chances of getting
- credit cards, loans, and mortgages;
- car financing,
- gas and electricity monthly payments,
- mobile phone contracts,
- insurance monthly payments, and
- property rentals

---

[1] http://www.experian.co.uk/consumer/experian-credit-report.html.
[2] Experian UK. Permission Granted on 11th July 2018 P27/35

## HOW DOES A CREDIT SCORE WORK?

Whenever you apply for credit, the lender will check your borrowing history and how you typically repay money you've borrowed. This happens when you apply for credit such as a loan, credit card, mortgage, car finance, and even a mobile phone contract.

They'll look at your credit history, which is based on your credit report and will show things like if you have a mortgage, how much you owe on credit cards, and whether you've missed payments in the past.

This is combined with the other information you fill in on the credit application form, as well as past information they've got on you (for example, if you're an existing customer). The lender will then decide if it would like to lend you money.

Each lender uses slightly different lending criteria, so make sure you look around for a deal that you're more likely to be accepted for, as well as being better suited to you and your credit history.

## WHAT DOES YOUR EXPERIAN CREDIT SCORE MEAN FOR YOU?

The Experian Credit Score runs from 0 to 999 and is based on the information in your Experian Credit Report. The higher your score, the greater the chance you have of getting the best credit deals.

The Experian Credit Score categories are shown below.

Excellent: 961–999
You should get the best credit cards, loans, and mortgages (but there are no guarantees).

Good: 881–960
You should get most credit cards, loans, and mortgages, but the very best deals may reject you.

Fair: 721–880
You might get OK interest rates, but your credit limits may not be very high.

Poor: 561–720
You might be accepted for credit cards, loans, and mortgages, but they may have higher interest rates.

Very Poor: 0–560
You're more likely to be rejected for most credit cards, loans, and mortgages that are available.

## WHAT IS A CREDIT REPORT?

A credit report details your personal credit history for accounts you've had in the last six years, including mortgages, credit cards, overdrafts, loans, mobile phone contracts and even some utilities such as gas, electricity, and water. If you're over eighteen and have taken out credit before, a credit reference agency is likely to hold a credit report on you.

*How do lenders use your credit report?*

A credit report gives insight into your credit accounts, repayment records, and how well you're coping with your finances.

Lenders usually have to tell you before they look at information from your credit report. They use it, along with what you've provided on your application form and information they might already have (if you're an existing customer), to help them decide whether or not to offer you credit. Usually they calculate their own credit score for your application.

*What's in your credit report?*

Your credit report contains information that helps lenders confirm your identity and assess whether you're a reliable borrower. This information includes the following.

Account Information

A view of credit accounts you've had and whether you've made repayments on time and in full. Items such as missed or late payments stay on your credit report for at least six years, as do court judgements for non-payment of debts, bankruptcies, and individual voluntary arrangements.

Financial Connections

A list of the people with whom you have a financial connection, such as a joint mortgage or bank account; they are known as your financial associates. Their credit history doesn't appear in your credit report. However, when you apply for credit, lenders are able to look at their credit history also because their circumstances could affect your ability to repay what you owe.

Address Details

A view of electoral roll information for your current address and previous addresses you provide when you apply. It also contains details of any other addresses you've been linked to in the past, such as those you've given to lenders on application forms.

## WHERE DOES THE INFORMATION IN YOUR CREDIT REPORT COME FROM?

The information in your credit report comes from two major sources:
- Public information. This includes electoral roll information and court judgements.
- Credit history information. Many lenders share information on what you owe and whether you've paid on time. You agree to this as part of any application for credit. Some lenders only contribute information on accounts that have defaulted, but these days most share monthly updates on all customers.

## WHEN SHOULD YOU CHECK YOUR CREDIT REPORT?

- If you're changing job or moving home
- If you're applying for credit
- If you're worried about ID fraud

## HOW TO IMPROVE YOUR CREDIT SCORE

With a higher credit score, you've got more chance of being accepted for credit at the best rates. A high credit rating can mean you'll get a better deal on a credit card, get a lower rate on a loan, and pay less interest on your mortgage, meaning it can save you money. Your Experian Credit Score is based on information in your Experian Credit Report and gives you an indication of how lenders may view you.

So how do you get a good credit rating? Follow my step-by-step guide.

1. Prove where you live.

Get on the electoral roll. This should be easy to do if you're a British or EU citizen. Lenders will check your name and address to prove that you live where you say you do. You can do this even if you are still living at home with parents or sharing student accommodation. This makes it easier for banks and financial institutions to confirm your identity.

2. Start to build credit history.

Having accounts such as a bank account could really help. Initially, taking out a new account might see your score reduce a little, but managing it well should help to improve your Experian Credit Score whilst building your credit history. A bank account with an overdraft facility is a form of credit and can show that you can keep within its spending limits.

3. Have some responsible credit.

Lenders typically like to see previous borrowing history. Taking out smaller forms of credit like a mobile phone contract, store card, or credit card could be easier to get accepted for. If you manage them well, they should show that you can pay bills responsibly and on time each month.

4. Consider closing unused accounts.

Consider closing unused credit accounts if you no longer require them. Lenders can take into account the credit limits available to you, not just what you currently owe. It could be better to have fewer, well-managed accounts, as well as long-standing accounts with good histories.

5. Space out credit applications.

Applying for lots of credit can suggest you are overly reliant on credit to supplement your income. If you can, aim for no more than one application for credit in a three-month period. This could be applying for a credit card, debit card, mortgage, or a car finance deal.

6. Aim to have your credit accounts for a long time.

Having new credit accounts may result in a decrease to your Experian Credit Score. However, as your accounts get older, having multiple accounts which you are managing well could have a positive effect on your Experian Credit Score.

7. Aim to have a good amount of available credit.

Your available credit is the difference between your outstanding balance and your credit limit. If you have low available credit, or a large number of your accounts are using above 50 per cent of your available credit, banks and financial institutions may think you're struggling to manage your finances.

8. Try not to miss payments.

Any missed payments in the last six years will have a negative effect on your Experian Credit Score. As your late payments become older, they reduce the negative effect on your Experian Credit Score.

9. Try to avoid delinquent and defaulted accounts.

Accounts become delinquent when you're late on payment. Accounts are defaulted when the borrower fails to repay the loan as scheduled in the initial agreement. Defaulted accounts will drop off your credit report after six years so long as they are satisfied.

10. Try to avoid or resolve CCJs, IVAs, or Scottish Trust Deeds.

County court judgements (CCJs), bankruptcy, individual voluntary arrangements (IVAs), and Scottish trust deeds will have a negative effect on your Experian Credit Score for six years from the date the entry was recorded. These records should not appear on your credit report after six years as long as they have been settled or discharged.

11. Protect your identity.

Look out for unfamiliar or suspicious entries in your report, such as an account you didn't open, a sudden surge in the amount you owe, or new credit applications you didn't make. They could mean you're a victim of identity fraud.

12. Improve your credit score if you've lived abroad.

If you have a credit history from a previous country, some lenders may be willing to take this into account when deciding whether to do business with you. You'll need to get it from the credit reference agency in that country and share it with the lender, but it could be a big help.

# WHAT THE RICH DO WITH THEIR MONEY

The rich are getting richer and the poor are getting poorer due to their mindsets. Because of the mindset of rich people, they think and act differently. For example, the things they buy are different from the things poor people will buy.

Income is money you bring in, and expenditure is money you spend. These two words are used by the poor, the middle class, and the rich in the same way. Liability is something that costs you, and asset is something that pays you. Asset is not your car, house, or something expensive that you own; it's something that pays you (i.e., you get income from your asset). The rich see assets in a totally different way than the poor.

The difference between the rich and poor is all wrapped up in what they do with their money when they get paid. The poor buy a lot of unnecessary, expensive stuff that become a liability to them, such as expensive shoes, trainers, clothes, phones, big TVs, and a lot of on-sale goods. Their houses are cluttered with junk and inexpensive things. Their cars and garages are also full of junk. They even withdraw money from their income and spend it each month, depleting their funds. As fast as the money comes in, it will go out. It's very easy to be trapped in this way because everywhere we turn, there are nice things to buy. However, after living like this for some years of their working lives, they have nothing to show for it. The poor never allow their money to create more money. This is not wrong in any way, and no one can judge you for this, but it keeps the poor in a terrible cycle that is very hard to escape from. You have to be willing to change your habits.

Wealth creation is a recipe, and the reason people doesn't create wealth is because they don't know this recipe, or they never use the recipe given them.

It's amazing to know that the middle class think they are rich because they have a good-paying job, but what they buy with their income is what makes them stuck in the middle and unable to move on. The middle class may own the homes they live in, which in financial terms is a liability, not an asset. They pay for vacations with credit cards, which again is a liability to them and adds to their monthly expenditure. They keep buying liabilities that cost them every month, and then they are trapped by the very things they bought to make them happy. These people get stressed out when they run out of money and have to pay for the kids' schools or next vacation, or when their cars break down. In time, they will add these expenditures to their credit card bills. Wealth creation is the creation of assets and not liabilities. It is important to note that you can make a lot of money but still be a poor person because of how you spend it.

For the rich and wealthy, instead of spending unnecessarily, they use their money to buy assets that will pay them or be reinvested into buying more assets, which makes them more money. The assets they hold make them more money instead of using their time and energy. The assets are stocks and shares, bonds, and real estate. The rich buy assets that pay them dividends. They buy bonds that pay them every month, semi-annually, or annually. They buy real estate that pays them every month. The house you own but live in is a liability, whereas a house you let out for rental income is an asset and gives you guaranteed income.

Education is also an asset that the rich invest in because it teaches them how to do something to give them more income. There's an adage that says, "If you think education is expensive, then you should see how expensive ignorance is."

But where the rich really make a difference is when they buy or create an asset that is a business, especially a business that will create passive income. When you build a business that can pay you even after you stop working, then you know you have created a true asset. This is what wealthy people do, and it doesn't even have to be a multinational corporation.

# WHAT IS INVESTMENT?

We normally save our money in the bank, and that is the surest way it can be safe and accessible. The money could grow depending on the percentage of interest paid. But if the applicable interest paid on your savings in not high enough to take care of inflation, your money will not grow that much, affecting your purchasing power in real terms.

If your objective for saving is growth, then you should consider investing as your best alternative. Investing helps you to grow your wealth in real terms over time. A lot of people invest their money in order to achieve major life goals like buying a house or car, paying for university fees, or putting money aside for their retirement.

The best and popular investments include bonds, shares, and real estate. Others are gold, oil, and collectibles such as artworks. No matter which type of investment you do, expectations are all the same: increasing in value so that when you sell, you can make a profit.

The potential in investing is higher than saving your money in the bank, but investing also has its pitfalls because it never guarantees you will make a profit. The future is uncertain, and some people even lose money. Some investments are safer than others, but all of them involve uncertainty.

## RISK AND RETURN

When you invest, the amount of money you gain is called the return. This is expressed as a percentage of your initial investment. Let's say you buy a house for £100,000 and sell it a year later for £120,000. The £20,000 will be your return on investment. However, if you do not make enough return as expected, then it's called risk.

Unfortunately, risk is part of investment. If you want to have more return on your investment, you take on more risk. For example, if you are lending to someone whose track record of borrowing is to promptly pay back, you will accept a low return. However, if you are lending to someone with a bad record of borrowing, then you will expect a higher return to compensate for the fact that you might lose your money by the borrower not paying. This is often referred to as a risk-reward trade-off.

## INVESTING AND SAVING

Savings and investing are two ways of putting money away for the future, but they each have different objectives. Savings offer you lower risk and easy accessibility at a shorter notice. The chances of you losing money in a bank is extremely low, and even in the United Kingdom, the government offers depositor protection for savings known as a financial services compensation scheme. Savings comes with minimal risk and minimal returns, especially when rates are low. However, savings is rarely an effective way of building your wealth.

Investing has a different purpose, which is mainly to grow your money by putting it to use where it will potentially make a profit, such as buying shares in a company or placing your money in an investment fund. Be aware that investing has potential but does not guarantee you a profit, and you may even lose your money. The value of your investment is also subject to fluctuation on a daily basis, whereas savings in a bank does not unexpectedly change. You may have to pay a fee for most investments, and proceeds from investments are taxable, which eats into your investment.

## TYPES OF INVESTMENTS

Stocks, in the same way as shares and equity, allow individuals and companies or investors to buy stakes in a listed company. If there are 1,000,000 shares and you buy 1, you have bought a 1/1,000,000 share of it. A shareholder is an individual or a group who owns a certain percentage of the company. Even if you own a small percentage of shares in a successful business, you are entitled to a percentage of the company's profit. You will get dividends whether quarterly, semi-annually, or annually, and that will give you better returns in the longer term than if you save the money in a bank. You could also sell part of your shares to realise income. If the company makes money, you will make more money, and if they lose money, share prices will go down and your income from selling shares will be down as well. You should consider risk versus reward before investing your money.

## BONDS

There are corporate bonds and government bonds. Corporate bonds are bonds issued by a company, and government bonds are issued by the government.

Companies borrow to fund projects in order to help them grow, and governments borrow to cover the difference between how much they made through taxes and their expenditure. Whereas loan is one option of borrowing money, companies and governments have access to the bond market as well.

A bond is packaged into evenly sized mini loan agreements regarding what needs to be borrowed, and the bonds are sold to investors. This way of raising money has been in existence since ancient times.

## ALTERNATIVE INVESTMENTS

Diversification is the process of spreading your money across different types of investments. Diversification helps to spread risk because while some investments are doing poorly, others will be doing well. Spreading your risk helps to minimise losses. Investing in different forms of bonds and equities is a way of diversifying your portfolio, but the more experienced investors will add other things such as gold, real estate, oil, vintage wines, classic cars, and works of art. Alternative investments are difficult to understand and also require more money as a minimum investment than the usual stocks and shares; they are not suitable for people new to investment.

Two mainstream alternative investments are real estate (properties) and commodities such as sugar, gold, grains, cocoa, rice, corn, oats, livestock, precious metals, electricity, crude oil, oranges, and natural gas.

Are you planning on supplementing your income or building a retirement pot? What would you like from your investment?

## INVESTING FOR INCOME AND GROWTH: PREDICTABLE RETURNS VERSUS GROWING IN VALUE

The return investors seek for their investment comes in two types, growth and income. Growth is appreciation in capital when you sell an investment, or the returns you make when you sell an investment which is more than your initial investment or the price paid. Income is the money you receive from an investment whilst still in the investment contract, such as dividend or interest payment. This is a regular focus for investors as they seek better predictable returns. Many investments give you income and still grow, so there is no need to choose either. For example, a property can be rented for income and still appreciate in value to be later sold for profit. Shares pay dividends and have the potential for growth as well.

## RISK APPETITE: HOW MUCH UNCERTAINTY WOULD YOU COMFORTABLY ACCEPT?

Some investors have higher risk appetites than others and can accept market fluctuations no matter what happens. Others were not born that way. Some people are natural risk takers whereas others are more cautious about risk, so it depends on your risk-taking appetite or tolerance. Your understanding of the market, the stage of life you are at, and your financial circumstances can all influence your risk appetite. It's difficult to take risk, but it might be more ideal depending on what returns you expect from your investments.

It is important to note that if you are constantly worrying about the risk you have taken, then you probably have taken on too much. A big swing in the value of your investments might cause panic and make you regret your actions, but being too conservative might make you miss out on promising investments. If you are not sure about your risk tolerance, seek advice from a reputable financial advisor who can answer all the questions you have.

## LIFE STAGES: TIME, THE YOUNG INVESTOR'S FRIEND

You may have a lot of reasons for investing at many stages of life. For example, you may need funds for a wedding, children's education, and mortgage deposits, all in the short to medium term. But for a longer term, you will need retirement funds. Whilst early in life, you may not have enough money, and saving or investing in smaller regular and consistent amounts may boost your investment as you have more time to add and build on your investment portfolio because of the nature of the compounding effect over a long period of time. Investing from a younger age gives you the ability to take on more and higher risk investment because it will have time to correct itself when markets are not performing well, and you can hold on to investments for a longer time in spite of fluctuations. Investors in their twenties and thirties focus on shares due to their high potential for growth. At this early stage of your life, it is important to plan ahead and think about your retirement fund. Normally, employers will offer a retirement plan, but it may not be enough, and so you will have to contribute to this pension plan or find alternative ways of investing.

## LIFE STAGES: MIDLIFE

The time when your earning power begins to reach its peak is the midlife, and it runs for a decade before retirement. At midlife, you have a clearer idea of your financial goals for accumulating wealth and meeting financial obligations like mortgage payments or education fees. But at midlife, you may not have enough time left, so it's best to consider income-generating investments like bonds rather than shares. During midlife, you should seriously consider your retirement goals and find strategies to achieve them.

## LIFE STAGES: PRERETIREMENT INCOME

Protecting and maximising your funds at the retirement stage is key, and bonds will be the best product for your money because they are more stable and provide a fixed income. You should plan your retirement income as to how much you will require and will be able to withdraw each year. Chasing higher returns at this stage of your life is not usually advisable because you may lose money, and you won't have the stomach for higher risk investments. Your major priority at this stage is to protect your wealth.

## LIFE STAGES: POSTRETIREMENT INCOME

Your first priority during retirement is to protect your funds and ensure that you have enough income to last you for the rest of your life, including meeting future costs like healthcare. At this stage, the best investment is bonds. If you have excess cash, you may consider stocks and shares, but the beneficiary is your next of kin.

# A STURDY FLOW OF INCOME?

If your main purpose in investing is to receive a constant flow of income, then you need to select an investment designed for that purpose over a certain period of time. This is the best way to chase decent returns and at the same time protect your money from inflation through equities, dividends, bonds, property, and annuities.

When you invest in equities, you are supporting a company that has the potential to perform well, pay significant dividends, and share in profits with its shareholders. Many companies do well and continually improve on dividend payments, and share prices rise over a certain length of time. However, this type of investment is subject to fluctuations. This type of investment is highly volatile in response to market conditions and effects from other companies.

You can take dividends as income or reinvest in equities and for a longer term; the addition of dividends will increase the overall investment due to the power of compound interest.

Bonds offer fixed income from your lending to companies and government. Bonds pay a mark-up on top of your original investment at the end of a fixed term. However, bonds carry the risk of company failure and eventual default, movements in interest rates, and changes by the government. Value can decrease due to interest rates being cut, or they can increase due to interest rates rising.

For a buy-to-let property investment, you get income from rent and market value appreciation. Rent can be increased in line with inflation so you don't lose out. You can also invest in a property fund, but this type of investment can sometimes be difficult to deal in its units, or sell them at a reasonable price. It also carries the risk that information about the properties invested in the funds are unreliable.

Annuities are an income-generating contract sold by an insurance firm and are normally associated with retirement savings. This will give you an income for life, but the level of income is determined by the government through interest rates of bonds issued by the government at the time of purchase.

# WHAT ARE MUTUAL FUNDS?

Investor gurus have advised that some of the best forms of long-term investments are by stocks and shares and bonds through mutual funds. So what are mutual funds?

According to investor.gov,[3]

> A mutual fund is a company that pools money from many investors and invests the money in securities such as stocks, bonds, and short-term debt. The combined holdings of the mutual fund are known as its portfolio. Investors buy shares in mutual funds. Each share represents an investor's part ownership in the fund and the income it generates.

Mutual funds are very popular with investors because there is a fund manager who performs market research, selects securities, and monitors the fund's performance on

---

[3] https://www.investor.gov/investing-basics/investment-products/mutual-funds.

your behalf. You don't need to be an expert in investment to invest in mutual funds.

There is an adage that says, "Don't put your eggs in one basket." Mutual funds invest in a broad range of companies and industries. In doing so, if one company is not performing well, the others should be OK. This is called diversification of funds.

Mutual funds are set in a way that anyone can afford them because it sets a lower minimum amount for initial and subsequent investments. Mutual funds are also highly liquid—that is, the investor is allowed to redeem shares at any time if he or she wishes, based on current net asset value and any redemption fee.

## TYPES OF MUTUAL FUNDS

Mutual funds fall into four categories: stocks funds, money market funds, bond funds, and target date funds. Each type of mutual fund has different features, different risks, and different rewards.

By far, money market funds are the one with lower risks because by law, they can only invest in certain types of high-quality, short-term investments issued by the local government.

Bond funds give higher returns but are a bit riskier than money market funds. Because there are many different types of bonds, the risks and rewards of bond funds can vary dramatically, making it risky.

Stock funds invest in corporate stocks.[4] Not all stock funds are the same. Some examples are as follows.

1. Growth funds focus on stocks that may not pay a regular dividend but have potential for above-average financial gains.
2. Income funds invest in stocks that pay regular dividends.
3. Index funds track a particular market index such as the Standard & Poor's 500 Index.
4. Sector funds specialise in a particular industry segment.

Target date funds hold a mixture of assets, including bonds, stocks, and other types of investments. After a while, the mix will gradually shift according to the fund's strategy. This type of fund is ideal for investors or individuals with a set retirement date in mind.

## ADVANTAGES AND DISADVANTAGES OF MUTUAL FUNDS

Mutual funds have a lot of advantages. It is a managed fund with professional investment managers who diversify the portfolio to manage risk. Investors earn income through dividend payments from stocks or interest payments from bonds after all expenses have been deducted, which can also be reinvested.

Prices of securities can also gain value over time, and when the fund sells a security that had increased in value, it

---

[4] https://www.investor.gov/investing-basics/investment-products/mutual-funds.

is said that the fund has capital gains. This positive return is redistributed to investors at the end of the year minus any expenses.

The net asset value (NAV) of an investment can also increase in value after all expenditure is deducted; the value of the fund and the share price will increase. A higher NAV reflects a higher value of your investment.

Mutual funds also have disadvantages. The value of the securities can go down as well, hence affecting your investment. You may lose some of the money you invested or sometimes all of it. As market conditions change, dividend and interest payment may also be affected.

"A fund's past performance is not as important as you might think because past performance does not predict future returns. But past performance can tell you how volatile or stable a fund has been over a period of time. The more volatile the fund, the higher the investment risk."[5]

## MUTUAL FUNDS FEES

There are fees, costs, and taxes for running or managing mutual funds. These costs are passed down to investors in fees and expenses, which vary from fund to fund. A small difference in fees can mean a large difference in returns over time.

> For example, if you invested $10,000 in a fund with a 10% annual return, and annual operating

---

[5] https://www.investor.gov/investing-basics/investment-products/mutual-funds

expenses of 1.5%, after 20 years you would have roughly $49,725. If you invested in a fund with the same performance and expenses of 0.5%, after 20 years you would end up with $60,858. You can use a mutual fund cost calculator to calculate the overall cost of different mutual funds over time to see the real cost that will eat into your returns.[6]

## BUYING AND SELLING OF MUTUAL FUNDS

You can buy shares in mutual funds directly with the funds itself, or you can go through a broker for the fund instead of from other investors. The price that investors pay for the mutual fund is the fund's per share net asset value plus any fees charged at the time of purchase, such as sales loads. Shares in mutual funds are redeemable, meaning investors can sell shares back to the fund at any time, and the fund will pay up within seven days. However, it is always advisable to read the prospectus carefully before buying shares in a mutual fund because the prospectus contains information about the mutual fund's objectives, risks, expenses, and performance.

---

[6] https://www.investor.gov/investing-basics/investment-products/mutual-funds.

## Mutual Fund Companies Ranked by Assets Under Management [1]

| Ranked by AUM on 03/7/2017 | Company Name | Assets Under Management (AUM) in $ Billions | New Date | Company Website |
|---|---|---|---|---|
| 1 | Black Rock Funds | $5,100.00 | 12/31/2016 | https://www.blackrock.com |
| 2 | Vanguard | $3,200.00 | 2/7/2017 | https://investor.vanguard.com/corporate-portal/ |
| 3 | State Street Global Advisors | $2,470.00 | 12/31/2016 | https://www.ssga.com/resources/universal/index.html |
| 4 | Fidelity Investments | $2,130.00 | 12/31/2016 | https://www.fidelity.com |
| 5 | JP Morgan | $1,772.00 | 12/31/2016 | https://www.jpmorgan.com |
| 6 | BNY Mellon (Dreyfus) | $1,700.00 | 9/30/2016 | https://im.bnymellon.com/us/en/index.jsp |
| 7 | PIMCO | $1,470.00 | 12/31/2016 | www.pimco.co.uk |
| 9 | American Funds Investments/PIMCO | $1,400.00 | 1/31/2017 | https://americanfundsretirement.retire.americanfunds.com/about/funds/multi-fund-details.htm?gvaFundUnitClassId=904230 |
| 8 | Prudential Investments | $1,000.00 | 12/31/2016 | https://www.pru.co.uk/investments/ |
| 10 | TIAA (purchased Nuveen) | $907.00 | 12/31/2016 | https://www.nuveen.com/Home/Default.aspx |
| 11 | Natixis Global Associates | $897.00 | 12/31/2016 | https://www2.im.natixis.com/global/12501946448l9/Home |
| 12 | Invesco | $825.30 | 12/31/2016 | http://www.invesco.com/corporate |
| 13 | T Rowe Price | $810.80 | 12/31/2016 | https://www3.troweprice.com/usis/corporate/en/home.html |

| Mutual Fund Companies Ranked by Assets Under Management [1] | | | | |
|---|---|---|---|---|
| 14 | TD Ameritrade | $797.00 | 12/31/2016 | https://www.tdameritrade.com/home.page |
| 15 | AXA | $785.50 | 12/31/2016 | https://www.axa.com |
| 16 | Affiliated Managers Group (AMG) | $727.00 | 12/31/2016 | https://www.amg.com |
| 17 | Franklin Templeton | $720.00 | 12/31/2016 | https://www.franklintempleton.co.uk |
| 18 | Deutsche Asset Management | $715.00 | 1/25/2017 | https://deutscheam.com/en-gb/ |
| 19 | Legg Mason | $713.80 | 1/30/2017 | http://www.leggmason.co.uk/landing.aspx |
| 20 | Goldman Sachs Asset Management | $707.00 | 12/31/2016 | https://www.gsam.com |
| 21 | UBS | $645.00 | 12/31/2016 | https://www.ubs.com/global/en.html |
| 22 | Principal Financial Group | $591.60 | 12/31/2016 | https://www.principal.com |
| 23 | B of A Merrill Lynch | $564.00 | 9/30/2016 | https://www.bofaml.com/content/boaml/en_us/home.html |
| 24 | RBC Global Wealth (CAN) | $560.00 | 12/31/2016 | https://www.rbcwealthmanagement.com |
| 25 | Wells Fargo Advantage Funds | $482.00 | 12/31/2016 | https://www.wellsfargofunds.com |
| 26 | Alliance Bernstein | $480.00 | 12/31/2016 | https://www.alliancebernstein.com |
| 27 | Dimensional Fund Advisers | $460.00 | 12/31/2016 | https://www.dimensional.com |

| | Mutual Fund Companies Ranked by Assets Under Management [1] | | | |
|---|---|---|---|---|
| 28 | Columbia Management | $456.30 | 12/31/2016 | http://www.columbiathreadneedle.com |
| 29 | MFS Investment Management | $433.90 | 12/31/2016 | https://www.mfs.com |
| 30 | Morgan Stanley | $417.00 | 12/31/2016 | https://www.morganstanley.com |
| 31 | Lafayette Investments | $387.00 | 2/3/2017 | http://www.lafayetteinvestments.com |
| 32 | Aberdeen Asset Management (UK) | $374.00 | 1/31/2017 | http://www.aberdeen-asset.co.uk |
| 33 | Nomura Asset Management | $372.00 | 12/31/2016 | http://www.nomura.com |
| 34 | Federated Investors | $365.90 | 12/31/2016 | http://www.federatedinvestors.com/ |
| 35 | BNP Paribas | $363.90 | 12/31/2015 | http://www.bnpparibas.co.uk/en/ |
| 36 | The BlackStone Group | $360.00 | 12/31/2016 | https://www.blackstone.com |
| 37 | Eaton Vance Distributors | $354.30 | 12/31/2016 | https://www.eatonvance.com |
| 38 | AVIVA | $350.70 | 12/31/2016 | https://www.aviva.co.uk |
| 39 | Julius Baer Securities | $332.00 | 12/31/2016 | https://www.juliusbaer.com/global/en/home/ |
| 40 | Lizard Mgmt Group | $288.00 | 12/31/2016 | http://www.lizardinvestors.com |
| 41 | Charles Schwab | $280.00 | 12/31/2016 | https://www.schwab.com |
| 42 | Dodge & Cox | $259.00 | 12/31/2016 | https://www.dodgeandcox.com |

| | Mutual Fund Companies Ranked by Assets Under Management [1] | | | |
|---|---|---|---|---|
| 43 | Frank Russell Investments (Northwestern Mutual) | $244.00 | 6/30/2016 | https://russellinvestments.com/us/ |
| 44 | Pioneer Investments | $240.80 | 12/31/2016 | http://www.pioneerinvestments.co.uk |
| 45 | Oppenheimer Funds | $226.00 | 12/31/2016 | https://www.oppenheimerfunds.com |
| 46 | Neuberger Berman | $221.00 | 12/31/2016 | https://www.nb.com |
| 47 | Barring Capital Management | $217.80 | 12/31/2016 | https://www.barings.com |
| 48 | Voya (ING) | $217.00 | 12/31/2016 | https://www.voya.com |
| 49 | Janus Capital Group | $191.90 | 12/31/2016 | https://en-us.janushenderson.com |
| 50 | Apollo Management | $191.70 | 2/3/2017 | http://www.agm.com/Home.aspx |
| 51 | TCW Group | $185.20 | 12/31/2016 | https://www.tcw.com |
| 52 | Estancia Capital Mgmt | $182.70 | 12/31/2016 | https://www.estanciapartners.com |
| 53 | Ameriprise Financial | $178.00 | 6/30/2016 | https://www.ameriprise.com |
| 54 | Carlyle Group | $158.00 | 12/31/2016 | https://www.carlyle.com |
| 55 | Putnam Investments | $156.00 | 12/31/2016 | https://www.putnam.com/uk/ |
| 56 | Guggenheim Partners | $150.80 | 12/31/2016 | https://www.guggenheiminvestments.com |
| 57 | Lord Abbett & Co | $146.70 | 12/31/2016 | https://www.lordabbett.com/en.html |
| 58 | IGM Financial | $145.00 | 12/31/2016 | https://www.igmfinancial.com/en |

| Mutual Fund Companies Ranked by Assets Under Management [1] | | | | |
|---|---|---|---|---|
| 59 | American Century Investments (Nomura to buy 41%) | $137.00 | 12/31/2016 | https://corporate.americancentury.com/en.html |
| 60 | John Hancock Funds (CAN) | $135.00 | 12/31/2016 | http://www.jhinvestments.com/Welcome.aspx |
| 61 | USAA Investment Management | $128.00 | 12/31/2016 | http://www.advisorusaa.com |
| 62 | Aegon | $112.00 | 12/31/2016 | https://www.aegonassetmanagement.com/en/us/home/ |
| 63 | LPL Financial (Note: advisory funds only) | $112.00 | 12/31/2016 | https://lplfinancial.lpl.com |
| 64 | Oakmark Funds | $109.00 | 12/31/2016 | https://www.oakmark.com/oakmark.htm |
| 65 | The Hartford | $107.00 | 12/31/2016 | https://www.hartfordfunds.com/home.html |
| 66 | Doubleline | $106.00 | 12/31/2016 | https://doubleline.com |
| 67 | OakTree | $101.00 | 2/7/2017 | https://www.oaktreecapital.com |
| 68 | Ares Management | $99.00 | 12/31/2016 | https://www.aresmgmt.com |
| 69 | First Eagle Investment Management | $97.00 | 12/31/2016 | https://www.feim.com |
| 70 | Artisan Partners Financial | $96.80 | 12/31/2016 | https://www.artisanpartners.com |
| 71 | Robert W Baird & Co | $83.90 | 12/31/2016 | http://www.rwbaird.com |

| Mutual Fund Companies Ranked by Assets Under Management [1] | | | | |
|---|---|---|---|---|
| 72 | William Blair Funds | $82.00 | 9/30/2016 | https://www.williamblairfunds.com/default.fs |
| 73 | MAN Group | $80.70 | 9/30/2016 | https://www.man.com |
| 74 | Conning | $79.10 | 12/31/2016 | https://www.conning.com |
| 75 | TransAmerica Funds | $77.90 | 12/2/2016 | https://www.transamerica.com/individual/ |
| 76 | TPG Capital | $74.00 | 12/31/2016 | https://www.tpg.com |
| 77 | Fortress | $69.60 | 12/31/2016 | https://www.fortress.com |
| 78 | MacKenzie Investments (CAN) | $64.00 | 12/31/2016 | https://www.mackenzieinvestments.com |
| 79 | US Bancorp | $62.70 | 12/31/2016 | https://www.usbank.com/investments-wealth-management/investment-management.html |
| 80 | Thornburg Asset Management | $54.90 | 12/31/2016 | https://www.thornburg.com |
| 81 | MetLife | $53.40 | 12/31/2016 | https://www.metlife.co.uk |
| 82 | Credit Sussie | $52.50 | 12/31/2016 | https://www.credit-suisse.com/us/en/investment-banking.html |
| 83 | BMO Global Asset Group | $51.00 | 12/31/2016 | http://www.bmogam.com/home/ |
| 84 | Sterling Capital (BB&T) | $51.00 | 12/31/2016 | https://www.sterling-capital.com |
| 85 | Virtus Investment Partners | $45.40 | 12/31/2016 | https://www.virtus.com/#fund.all/class.all |
| 86 | Ivy Funds | $44.70 | 12/31/2016 | https://www.ivyinvestments.com |

| | Mutual Fund Companies Ranked by Assets Under Management [1] | | | |
|---|---|---|---|---|
| 87 | Waddell & Reed | $43.20 | 12/31/2016 | https://www.waddell.com |
| 88 | Gabelli Investors | $39.90 | 11/10/2016 | http://www.gabelli.com |
| 89 | Victory Capital | $35.80 | 12/31/2016 | https://www.vcm.com |
| 90 | AGF Management Limited | $34.00 | 2/3/2017 | https://www.agf.com/ca/en/index.jsp |
| 91 | Och-Ziff | $33.70 | 3/1/2017 | https://www.ozm.com |
| 92 | Cerberus Capital Management | $30.00 | 12/31/2016 | http://www.cerberuscapital.com |
| 93 | Davis Select Advisers | $28.90 | 12/31/2016 | http://davisadvisors.com |
| 94 | Matthews Asia Funds | $25.60 | 12/31/2016 | https://matthewsasia.com/portal.fs |
| 95 | Scout Investments | $23.20 | 12/31/2016 | http://scoutinv.com/portal.fs |
| 96 | Reams Asset Mgmt | $22.50 | 12/31/2016 | http://www.reamsasset.com |
| 97 | Sun Life Gobal Investments | $22.10 | 12/31/2016 | http://www.sunlifeglobalinvestments.com |
| 98 | Tweedy Browne Co | $18.40 | 12/31/2016 | http://www.tweedy.com |
| 99 | Royce Funds | $17.60 | 12/31/2016 | https://www.roycefunds.com |
| 100 | Touchstone Investments | $17.00 | 12/31/2016 | https://www.touchstoneinvestments.com |

# INVESTING IN PROPERTIES

Property investment is simply the purchase of future income streams from properties through rental yields for passive income and property appreciation, which is always inflation-proofed in good times.

Real estate investments give you monthly income through rentals, and they have tax advantages. The properties almost always gain value over time (capital gains), and banks will almost always lend you money for real estate.

One secret of property investment is to find property in areas where people are moving into. Such properties always appreciate, and you are guaranteed rent and capital gains. A city that has a higher growth is certain to carry on in the same way for the following years.

When planning to invest, the best thing is to watch the market trends and which are moving up, down, or sideways.

Another trick of property investment is to find an area that has experienced negative growth for a while but has the potential for positive growth. For example, when there is a planned development in the pipeline or a regeneration of the area, prices will start rising gradually.

Identify the area. When buying an investment property, make sure it is close to your house to avoid extra monitoring and management costs. The rule is area first, property second.

Find the right deal through research. Simply find a few properties and then research and evaluate them. If you don't find what you want, start again by finding one hundred properties and evaluate them. If you are not willing to go through one hundred deals to find one deal, you are bound to buy the wrong property.

Don't worry when the property looks ugly but has potential as an investment property. When everything else is right about a property, you simply spend a little bit of money to improve the look and quality. Fall in love with the area first before you look at the house.

You could buy properties off-plan through options, and by the time the property is completed, it is bound to have a higher value so that you can sell and take your profit.

Find the best brokers who support investors and not buyers, because they are able to advise you better.

Find property deals, negotiate a discount, find ways to finance the property deals, and manage the property by renting.

## WHY INVEST IN PROPERTIES?

Real estate is brick and mortar, which is a tangible asset and is more stable in nature. Real estate investments cut off the principal-agent relationship found in stocks and share investments, which depends on the integrity and competence of the investment managers and debtors. With real estates, you have 100 per cent control.

There is currently an acute shortage of rental properties in the market, so the opportunity to invest is vast, and there will always be a demand for rental properties because not everybody will be able to buy properties, especially with young people. Real estate investments provide a constant stream of income, meaning you can even quit your job to focus on real estate as your main business.

Real estate gives you tax advantages over other investments, and the property will almost always appreciate in value over time.

You can add value to a property by spotting a run-down property; renovate or develop it to create value out of nowhere.

It is known that property value doubles every ten years, so even when value goes down—for example, when there is a negative equity—there is no panic because the value will always creep up. All you need do is to give it time to readjust so that you will never lose with property investments.

## TYPES OF PROPERTY INVESTMENTS

Homes in multiple occupation, or HMOs, are private houses with three or more tenants living there, forming more than one household where toilets, bathrooms, and the kitchen are shared with other tenants. A large HMO is at least three storeys high with a minimum of five tenants living there.

HMOs, or multi-lets, can give you a rental yield that cannot be achieved with the standard buy-to-let. In the right areas, the demand for HMOs has always been higher. One positive thing about HMOs is that when a tenant moves out, you have other tenants who are still paying for their accommodation, so you don't lose out.

To embark on an investment in HMOs, you need to inquire from the local authority of the property as to the licensing requirements and the planning regulation.

However, as with all types of investments, you need to do thorough research. Read widely on the subject of HMOs. Speak with your local HMO officer, who has been employed by the local authority to help landlords.

Property flips are properties bought and sold in a period of twelve months. If you want to flip a property, do your homework really well and never buy at the maximum price because you need to consider closing cost, commission, insurances, taxes, and mortgage. It's best to use cash to renovate in order to make it competitive to sell because your cost will go down. Look at recent sale prices of comparable houses.

It is best to find houses not on the property market yet. Go straight to the owner, a bank auction, or a housing wholesaler for a good deal because once the house is listed, it will get pricey. The house should be right so that it won't need too much work. Your focus should be on the kitchen, bathrooms, and systems, which matter most to buyers. Also focus on good appliances and fixtures.

Commercial conversion is when a commercial property such as an office or workshop area is converted into residential dwellings and either flipped or rented. Before you get into commercial conversions, you have to know how the systems work. Have the right education, financial support, time, and team in place to take off. One benefit of commercial conversion is that the price of commercial properties is generally lower than that of residential properties. This is mainly due to oversaturation in the commercial property market. Another reason why commercial properties are cheaper is because they are often left for a longer period so that when it comes to sales, they always want to get rid of the property quickly—hence the lower prices.

Land development is altering the landscape in any number of ways, such as the following.

Changing landforms from a natural or seminatural state for a purpose such as housing.

Subdividing real estate into lots, typically for the purpose of building homes.

Real estate development or changing its purpose; for example, by converting an unused factory complex into a condominium.

Home building and containment are two of the most common and oldest types of development.

# INVESTMENTS

In a nutshell, in order to learn how to invest, follow Warren Buffet's annual letters, Mohnish Pabrai on Dhandho Investor, and Guy Spier on The Education of a Valued Investor.

To invest in a business, first understand the nature of the business and management, such as whether you share the same values with them. Always buy on a special offer or discount.

The best investments are in properties, stocks and shares, ISA, mutual funds, and bonds.

It is also important to note that investment is not only money related but also investment in people. Get out there and meet new people, network, and love one another.

Find something you're passionate about and focus on serving others' needs.

People are created to be givers and takers. There is more blessing in giving than receiving.

# HOW TO SAVE MONEY THE UNCONVENTIONAL WAY

Saving money the unconventional way is not about saving the money we make. It's about the percentage of money we keep without cutting back drastically on the way we live, as well as being disciplined and setting rules with what you already have or regularly receive.

Pay yourself first—at least 10 per cent of your income. If you do it the other way round and pay everybody else first and yourself last, then you are not going to get wealthy quickly enough. When you pay yourself first and only have that 90 per cent of your income left for all other expenditure, you are able to restrict yourself from overspending because you know once that money is finished, that's it.

If you keep all your money in one account, the likelihood that you will regularly access this money is great. The best thing to do to keep you away from some of the money is to have separate accounts for expenditure, investments, business, and savings. When you do this, you are able to restrict yourself from overspending.

If you are in debt, find creative ways to actively get out of debt because debt is very expensive and will prevent you from creating wealth.

Auditing your financial position is very important. You need to audit what comes into your account and what goes out of your account within ninety days. Be honest with where you are—that is, your income and expenditure within ninety days. Look at the difference: is it negative or positive? If it's negative, revisit your expenditure and make changes by reducing outgoing expenses.

Use money-saving apps that link to your account to instantly deduct a certain percentage of the money into your investment or savings account.

Financial IQ is something you don't learn in school. I will say you should constantly educate yourself on how to be rich with books like *Money Master the Game* by Tony Robbins, *Rich Dad Poor Dad* by Robert Kiyosaki, *The Cold Hard Truth on Men, Women and Money* by Kevin O'Leary, and *I Will Teach You to Be Rich* by Ramit Sethi.

# SMART MONEY, WISE KIDS—LET'S NOT FORGET OUR CHILDREN

The best thing we can do for our kids is to teach them the principles of money and how to handle it. So how do we raise children in a way that they become wise about money? It's good to raise good kids, but it's also important to raise kids who become adults and leave their parents' home and are not burden to their parents.

You have to teach your children that they don't own anything, but the Supreme Being owns it all. If you think it's all about you and you own it all, then you become selfish. But if you understand that anything you own is for the Supreme Being, it changes your thinking. If you understand this principle at any age, it changes your life and the way you handle money, especially other people's money. You will handle other people's money better than the money you own yourself. When you realise you don't own it but are just a manager, and the Supreme Being owns it all, it will put a responsibility on you to manage well the blessings He has put in your hands. Do not allow kids to be entitled to anything; it makes them arrogant and selfish.

Teach them the value of work, and if you don't work, you will not get any money. Do not simply hand money to kids; they will think it's easier to get it than to work for it. Give them commission for doing their chores or something specific. They have to link together hard work, earnings, and money. When you work, save and buy what you want. They'll learn a lot in life like sacrifice, patience, and delayed gratification, and they will become good stewards of their money.

Teach your kids to give from the money they earn from their own pockets. This will give them a solid foundation.

Teach kids that contentment is great gain. They have to be content with the little they have, and they will become very grateful in life. Grateful people are nice; ungrateful people are ugly. Teach them humility and not humiliation. When they are humble, they become content with the little they have.

# THE POWER OF COMPOUND INTEREST[7]

With a little bit of interest and a lot of time, compound interest can work magic. Compound interest may be considered one of the powerful concepts in finance. It is reinvesting earned interest back into the principal of an investment. Earning interest on top of interest increases the principal, resulting in exponential growth over time. Exponential growth is the acceleration of growth in the investment's principal. Exponential growth is letting interest compound over time.

Suppose two people plan to invest £10,000 in an investment for thirty years but one of them plans to withdraw interest at the end of each year whereas the other plans to reinvest the interest and let it compound for the rest of the thirty years. Fast-forward to thirty years at an interest or growth rate of 5 per cent annually, and at the end of the thirty years, the one who reinvested the interest would more than double the investment. Compounding over a long period of time can lead to exponential growth.

---

[7] https://www.thecalculatorsite.com/finance/calculators/compoundinterestcalculator.php.

Savers are investors because if you save money, you also learn to invest money. For example, a £100 a month invested in decent growth stocks in mutual funds from age thirty to age seventy will give you over £1,000,000.

Compound interest works best when you start investing early or are reinvesting earnings in the form of capital gains or dividends. Some brokers may allow you to automatically reinvest earnings or simply buy more investments with capital gains and dividends. Compounding works only if you are earning interest on your investments, but remember that investments in stocks and shares are prone to fluctuations, and you may lose some money, so do not overindulge and take too much risk. Large losses can be reduced by allocating your portfolio across different asset classes such as stocks, bonds, commodities, and currencies. Resist the temptation to take excessive risks with the hopes of earning fast money because with compound interest, slow and steady is a better approach.

The below calculation is based on a £500 one-time base deposit and £500 monthly top-up thereafter with an interest rate of 8 per cent over a period of forty years. As you can see below, between the thirty-third and thirty-fourth year, the accumulation enters into a million and carries on. Between the thirty-four and the fortieth year, an additional £769,000 is added with the same monthly deposits.

Exhibit 2 is a base deposit of £1,000 plus a regular monthly top-up of £100 at a rate of 8 per cent for forty years.

Both exhibit 1 and 2 have interest compounded monthly.

Some people complain about the discipline of saving for forty years, but what we should understand is that planning and investing for your pensions should not take less than thirty to forty years if we want to have financial freedom in our old age.

Exhibit 1

| Year | Year Deposits | Year Interest | Total Deposits | Total Interest | Balance |
|---|---|---|---|---|---|
| 1 | £6,000.00 | £307.96 | £6,500.00 | £307.96 | £6,807.96 |
| 2 | £6,000.00 | £831.52 | £12,500.00 | £1,139.48 | £13,639.48 |
| 3 | £6,000.00 | £1,398.53 | £18,500.00 | £2,538.02 | £21,038.02 |
| 4 | £6,000.00 | £2,012.61 | £24,500.00 | £4,550.62 | £29,050.62 |
| 5 | £6,000.00 | £2,677.65 | £30,500.00 | £7,228.27 | £37,728.27 |
| 6 | £6,000.00 | £3,397.89 | £36,500.00 | £10,626.16 | £47,126.16 |
| 7 | £6,000.00 | £4,177.91 | £42,500.00 | £14,804.08 | £57,304.08 |
| 8 | £6,000.00 | £5,022.67 | £48,500.00 | £19,826.75 | £68,326.75 |
| 9 | £6,000.00 | £5,937.55 | £54,500.00 | £25,764.30 | £80,264.30 |
| 10 | £6,000.00 | £6,928.36 | £60,500.00 | £32,692.66 | £93,192.66 |
| 11 | £6,000.00 | £8,001.41 | £66,500.00 | £40,694.07 | £107,194.07 |
| 12 | £6,000.00 | £9,163.52 | £72,500.00 | £49,857.58 | £122,357.58 |
| 13 | £6,000.00 | £10,422.08 | £78,500.00 | £60,279.66 | £138,779.66 |

| 14 | £6,000.00 | £11,785.11 | £84,500.00 | £72,064.77 | £156,564.77 |
| --- | --- | --- | --- | --- | --- |
| 15 | £6,000.00 | £13,261.26 | £90,500.00 | £85,326.03 | £175,826.03 |
| 16 | £6,000.00 | £14,859.94 | £96,500.00 | £100,185.97 | £196,685.97 |
| 17 | £6,000.00 | £16,591.30 | £102,500.00 | £116,777.27 | £219,277.27 |
| 18 | £6,000.00 | £18,466.37 | £108,500.00 | £135,243.64 | £243,743.64 |
| 19 | £6,000.00 | £20,497.06 | £114,500.00 | £155,740.70 | £270,240.70 |
| 20 | £6,000.00 | £22,696.31 | £120,500.00 | £178,437.01 | £298,937.01 |
| 21 | £6,000.00 | £25,078.09 | £126,500.00 | £203,515.10 | £330,015.10 |
| 22 | £6,000.00 | £27,657.55 | £132,500.00 | £231,172.65 | £363,672.65 |
| 23 | £6,000.00 | £30,451.11 | £138,500.00 | £261,623.76 | £400,123.76 |
| 24 | £6,000.00 | £33,476.54 | £144,500.00 | £295,100.30 | £439,600.30 |
| 25 | £6,000.00 | £36,753.07 | £150,500.00 | £331,853.37 | £482,353.37 |
| 26 | £6,000.00 | £40,301.55 | £156,500.00 | £372,154.93 | £528,654.93 |
| 27 | £6,000.00 | £44,144.56 | £162,500.00 | £416,299.49 | £578,799.49 |
| 28 | £6,000.00 | £48,306.53 | £168,500.00 | £464,606.02 | £633,106.02 |
| 29 | £6,000.00 | £52,813.95 | £174,500.00 | £517,419.97 | £691,919.97 |
| 30 | £6,000.00 | £57,695.48 | £180,500.00 | £575,115.45 | £755,615.45 |
| 31 | £6,000.00 | £62,982.17 | £186,500.00 | £638,097.63 | £824,597.63 |

| | | | | | |
|---|---|---|---|---|---|
| 32 | £6,000.00 | £68,707.66 | £192,500.00 | £706,805.29 | £899,305.29 |
| 33 | £6,000.00 | £74,908.36 | £198,500.00 | £781,713.64 | £980,213.64 |
| 34 | £6,000.00 | £81,623.71 | £204,500.00 | £863,337.36 | £1,067,837.36 |
| 35 | £6,000.00 | £88,896.44 | £210,500.00 | £952,233.79 | £1,162,733.79 |
| 36 | £6,000.00 | £96,772.79 | £216,500.00 | £1,049,006.59 | £1,265,506.59 |
| 37 | £6,000.00 | £105,302.89 | £222,500.00 | £1,154,309.47 | £1,376,809.47 |
| 38 | £6,000.00 | £114,540.97 | £228,500.00 | £1,268,850.44 | £1,497,350.44 |
| 39 | £6,000.00 | £124,545.81 | £234,500.00 | £1,393,396.25 | £1,627,896.25 |
| 40 | £6,000.00 | £135,381.05 | £240,500.00 | £1,528,777.30 | £1,769,277.30 |

Regular Deposit Calculation

Base amount: £500.00

Interest Rate: 8%

Effective Annual Rate: 8.3%

Calculation period: 40 years

Exhibit 2

| Year | Year Deposits | Year Interest | Total Deposits | Total Interest | Balance |
|---|---|---|---|---|---|
| 1 | £1,200.00 | £136.29 | £2,200.00 | £136.29 | £2,336.29 |
| 2 | £1,200.00 | £247.20 | £3,400.00 | £383.50 | £3,783.50 |
| 3 | £1,200.00 | £367.32 | £4,600.00 | £750.82 | £5,350.82 |
| 4 | £1,200.00 | £497.41 | £5,800.00 | £1,248.22 | £7,048.22 |
| 5 | £1,200.00 | £638.29 | £7,000.00 | £1,886.52 | £8,886.52 |
| 6 | £1,200.00 | £790.87 | £8,200.00 | £2,677.38 | £10,877.38 |
| 7 | £1,200.00 | £956.11 | £9,400.00 | £3,633.50 | £13,033.50 |
| 8 | £1,200.00 | £1,135.07 | £10,600.00 | £4,768.56 | £15,368.56 |
| 9 | £1,200.00 | £1,328.88 | £11,800.00 | £6,097.44 | £17,897.44 |
| 10 | £1,200.00 | £1,538.77 | £13,000.00 | £7,636.21 | £20,636.21 |
| 11 | £1,200.00 | £1,766.09 | £14,200.00 | £9,402.30 | £23,602.30 |
| 12 | £1,200.00 | £2,012.27 | £15,400.00 | £11,414.57 | £26,814.57 |
| 13 | £1,200.00 | £2,278.89 | £16,600.00 | £13,693.46 | £30,293.46 |
| 14 | £1,200.00 | £2,567.63 | £17,800.00 | £16,261.09 | £34,061.09 |

| 15 | £1,200.00 | £2,880.35 | £19,000.00 | £19,141.44 | £38,141.44 |
| --- | --- | --- | --- | --- | --- |
| 16 | £1,200.00 | £3,219.01 | £20,200.00 | £22,360.45 | £42,560.45 |
| 17 | £1,200.00 | £3,585.79 | £21,400.00 | £25,946.24 | £47,346.24 |
| 18 | £1,200.00 | £3,983.01 | £22,600.00 | £29,929.24 | £52,529.24 |
| 19 | £1,200.00 | £4,413.19 | £23,800.00 | £34,342.44 | £58,142.44 |
| 20 | £1,200.00 | £4,879.09 | £25,000.00 | £39,221.52 | £64,221.52 |
| 21 | £1,200.00 | £5,383.65 | £26,200.00 | £44,605.17 | £70,805.17 |
| 22 | £1,200.00 | £5,930.09 | £27,400.00 | £50,535.26 | £77,935.26 |
| 23 | £1,200.00 | £6,521.88 | £28,600.00 | £57,057.14 | £85,657.14 |
| 24 | £1,200.00 | £7,162.79 | £29,800.00 | £64,219.93 | £94,019.93 |
| 25 | £1,200.00 | £7,856.90 | £31,000.00 | £72,076.83 | £103,076.83 |
| 26 | £1,200.00 | £8,608.62 | £32,200.00 | £80,685.45 | £112,885.45 |
| 27 | £1,200.00 | £9,422.73 | £33,400.00 | £90,108.18 | £123,508.18 |
| 28 | £1,200.00 | £10,304.41 | £34,600.00 | £100,412.59 | £135,012.59 |
| 29 | £1,200.00 | £11,259.27 | £35,800.00 | £111,671.86 | £147,471.86 |
| 30 | £1,200.00 | £12,293.38 | £37,000.00 | £123,965.25 | £160,965.25 |
| 31 | £1,200.00 | £13,413.33 | £38,200.00 | £137,378.58 | £175,578.58 |
| 32 | £1,200.00 | £14,626.23 | £39,400.00 | £152,004.80 | £191,404.80 |

| | | | | |
|---|---|---|---|---|
| 33 | £1,200.00 | £15,939.80 | £40,600.00 | £167,944.60 | £208,544.60 |
| 34 | £1,200.00 | £17,362.39 | £41,800.00 | £185,306.99 | £227,106.99 |
| 35 | £1,200.00 | £18,903.06 | £43,000.00 | £204,210.05 | £247,210.05 |
| 36 | £1,200.00 | £20,571.61 | £44,200.00 | £224,781.66 | £268,981.66 |
| 37 | £1,200.00 | £22,378.64 | £45,400.00 | £247,160.30 | £292,560.30 |
| 38 | £1,200.00 | £24,335.65 | £46,600.00 | £271,495.95 | £318,095.95 |
| 39 | £1,200.00 | £26,455.10 | £47,800.00 | £297,951.05 | £345,751.05 |
| 40 | £1,200.00 | £28,750.46 | £49,000.00 | £326,701.51 | £375,701.51 |

Regular Deposit Calculation
Base amount: £1,000.00
Interest Rate: 8%
Effective Annual Rate: 8.3%
Calculation period: 40 years

| Income: What money do you receive? | | | |
|---|---|---|---|
| If income is variable enter an average | Amount | How often? | Per calendar month |
| Your wage | | | |
| You partner's wage | | | |
| Part-time wages | | | |
| Child benefit | | | |
| Rent or board received | | | |
| State pension | | | |
| Private pensions | | | |
| Pension credit | | | |
| Employment and Support Allowance (ESA) | | | |
| Jobseeker's Allowance (JSA) | | | |
| Child Support or CSA | | | |
| Disability Living Allowance (DLA) | | | |
| Income Support | | | |
| Working Tax Credit | | | |
| Child Tax Credit | | | |

| Housing Benefit | | | | | | |
|---|---|---|---|---|---|---|
| | | | | | | |
| | | | | | TOTAL INCOME | £0 |
| | | | | | | |

## Expenditure: Your living costs

| Enter the total amount you pay including towards arrears you may have | Payment amount (£) | How often? (e.g., weekly, monthly) | Average per calendar month |
|---|---|---|---|
| **Housing and Utility Bills** | | | |
| Rent or Mortgage | | | |
| Secured loan (other than your mortgage) | | | |
| Mortgage endowment premium | | | |
| Service charge or ground rent | | | |
| Water | | | |
| Council tax | | | |
| Gas | | | |
| Electricity | | | |
| Other household fuels (oil, coal etc) | | | |
| **Household Services** | | | |
| Buildings and contents insurance | | | |
| Telephone and internet | | | |
| TV licence | | | |
| Satellite or cable TV | | | |
| Repairs, service contracts | | | |

| | | | |
|---|---|---|---|
| Appliance rental | | | |
| Child support paid by you | | | |
| Childcare | | | |
| Life insurance and private pension | | | |
| Medical or accident insurance | | | |
| **Travel** | | | |
| Spares and servicing | | | |
| Road tax | | | |
| Car insurance | | | |
| Breakdown cover | | | |
| Fuel and parking | | | |
| Public transport | | | |
| **Food and Housekeeping** | | | |
| Food, toiletries and cleaning products | | | |
| School meals | | | |
| Meals at work | | | |
| Pets (food and insurance) | | | |
| Clothing and footwear | | | |

| Other Services | | |
|---|---|---|
| School trips and activities | | |
| Medicines and prescriptions | | |
| Dentist and opticians | | |
| Hairdressing | | |
| Professional, Education, or union fees | | |
| Laundry or dry cleaning | | |
| Personal and Leisure | | |
| Newspapers and magazines | | |
| Sports, hobbies, and entertainment | | |
| Children's pocket money | | |
| Church or charity donations | | |
| Sundries and emergencies | | |
| Other Costs | | |
| | **Total Expenditure** | |

Assets: What do you own?

| Type of asset | | Estimated value |
|---|---|---|
| | | |
| | | |
| | | |
| | | |
| Total Assets | | £0 |

Court payments

| Type of court order | Amount owed | Usual payment | How often? | Per calendar month |
|---|---|---|---|---|
| County Court judgment (CCJ) | £2,000.00 | £17.50 | Weekly | £76 |
| | | | | |
| | | | | |
| | | | | |
| | | | | |
| Total Court Debt | £0 | Total Court Payments | | £0 |

Debts: Who do you owe money to? (This could include rent arrears, gas or electricity, credit and store cards, bank loans, etc.)

| Name of organisation or lender | Type of debt | Amount owed | Usual payment | How often? | Per calendar month |
|---|---|---|---|---|---|
| *Example: Barclays Bank* | *Overdraft* | *£1,000.00* | *£100.00* | *Monthly* | *£100* |
|  |  |  |  |  |  |
|  |  |  |  |  |  |
|  |  |  |  |  |  |
|  |  |  |  |  |  |
|  |  |  |  |  |  |
|  |  |  |  |  |  |
|  |  |  |  |  |  |
|  |  |  |  |  |  |
|  |  |  |  |  |  |
|  | Total Debt | £0 |  | Total Debt Payments | £0 |

Bible Verses on Finances

Proverbs 10:15 King James Version
The rich man's wealth is his strong city: the destruction of the poor is their poverty.

Philippians 4:19 King James Version
But my God shall supply all your need according to his riches in glory by Christ Jesus.

Ecclesiastes 11:1–6 King James Version
Cast thy bread upon the waters: for thou shalt find it after many days. Give a portion to seven, and also to eight; for thou knowest not what evil shall be upon the earth. If the clouds be full of rain, they empty themselves upon the earth: and if the tree fall toward the south, or toward the north, in the place where the tree falleth, there it shall be. He that observeth the wind shall not sow; and he that regardeth the clouds shall not reap. As thou knowest not what is the way of the spirit, nor how the bones do grow in the womb of her that is with child: even so thou knowest not the works of God who maketh all. In the morning sow thy seed, and in the evening withhold not thine hand: for thou knowest not whether shall prosper, either this or that, or whether they both shall be alike good.

Psalm 35:27 King James Version
Let them shout for joy, and be glad, that favour my righteous cause: yea, let them say continually, Let the Lord be magnified, which hath pleasure in the prosperity of his servant.

Malachi 3:10 King James Version

Bring ye all the tithes into the storehouse, that there may be meat in mine house, and prove me now herewith, saith the Lord of hosts, if I will not open you the windows of heaven, and pour you out a blessing, that there shall not be room enough to receive it.

1 Timothy 6:10 King James Version

For the love of money is the root of all evil: which while some coveted after, they have erred from the faith, and pierced themselves through with many sorrows.

Proverbs 22:7 King James Version

The rich ruleth over the poor, and the borrower is servant to the lender.

Acts 20:35 King James Version

I have shewed you all things, how that so labouring ye ought to support the weak, and to remember the words of the Lord Jesus, how he said, It is more blessed to give than to receive.

# GLOSSARY OF INFORMATION

Find a financial or legal expert rated and reviewed by people like you
https://www.vouchedfor.co.uk

# ENDNOTES

1  Top 100 Mutual Funds in the World, 2017
   http://mutualfunddirectory.org/latest-directory-ranking-here/

www.ingramcontent.com/pod-product-compliance
Lightning Source LLC
Chambersburg PA
CBHW020446220526
45464CB00002B/884